OFF THE LEASH

Matthew Sturgis, author of the highly acclaimed *1992 and All This*, has written several books about cats, and even a book on Gazza. This, however, is his first Royal Dog book. He lives in London – and in hope of a knighthood.

Off the Leash

My Life as a Royal Corgi

as told to
Matthew Sturgis

Hodder & Stoughton

A CIP catalogue record for this title is available
from the British Library

ISBN 0–340–63414–7

Typeset by Avocet Typeset, Brill, Aylesbury, Bucks
Printed and bound in Great Britain by
Mackays of Chatham PLC, Chatham, Kent

Hodder and Stoughton
A division of Hodder Headline PLC
338 Euston Road
London NW1 3BH

In Memoriam
Moon
et
Stella

OUR ROYAL PEDIGREE

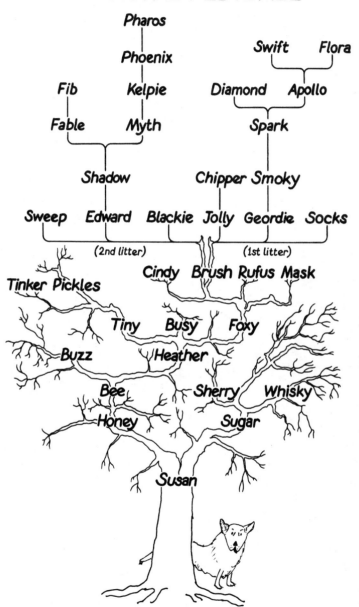

Foreword

[*not*]

by

His Royal Highness The Prince of Wales

Over the years I have penned forewords to many books. It is – I think I can say without boasting – one of the things I am rather good at. Nevertheless almost all of the publications I have graced with my seal of approval have been flippant or foolish, if not actually ridiculous: *The Goon Show Scripts*, *The Giles Annual* (1973), *The Further Adventures of Ranulph Twisleton-Wykeham-Fiennes*.

So it is a particular pleasure to be asked to write a few lines of introduction to a book so manifestly important and serious as this one.

These memoirs constitute, I believe, a unique historical record. They give an insight, at once penetrating and affectionate, into the Royal Family at a time of flux and transition. They speak with both candour and knowledge – qualities rare in most other so-called royal books (not that I read them).

I earnestly urge all those interested in the future of the monarchy not only to read *Off the Leash* but also to buy several extra copies to give to their friends, relatives and servants. It is a book that seems destined – even before publication – to become a classic.

Charles

Contents

OFF THE LEASH

Introduction

All those connected with the Royal Family (and few are more closely connected with them than I) have felt the sting in recent years of much of the hurtful and ill-informed gossip that has appeared in the Press.

The picture that has been presented of a hapless, out-of-touch group of loons, drifting from one embarrassing disaster to the next, is almost so distorted as not to merit the dignity of correction.

Nevertheless I have been persuaded (by my publishers and several Sunday papers) that the picture should be rectified. And as one who has lived on intimate terms with the Royal Family for over a decade I have sought to do so in these pages.

My memoirs of the Royal Household are an attempt to set the record straight. The home life of the Windsors is a subject famously open to speculation and even pure invention, but my reminiscences have the unique virtue of being taken down at first hand. I was there.

And you, as you read these pages, can be there too.

PART ONE

Our Royal Pedigree

A proud and ancient strain

The Royal Corgis are a proud and ancient strain. I can trace my own lineage back, through the mists of time, to 1944. That was the year when Susan, a splendid Pembrokeshire bitch, was given to the Queen as an eighteenth-birthday present. I, and most of the other corgis presently in the royal entourage, am descended from this great matriarch. We owe her everything: our thick, lustrous orange coats, our finely pointed ears, our white spats, our dark bright eyes – our place beside the throne.

It is not to be thought, however, that Susan was the first Royal Corgi. No. That singular honour belonged to Dookie. Dookie was introduced into the Royal Household in 1933 by the future George VI (then Duke of York). With his commanding bark and aristocratic air Dookie was an object of universal respect and admiration. He converted the Windsors to the Joy of Corgis. And it has to be said that the consideration shown him by George VI and his wife (the current Queen Mother) converted corgis to the Joy of the Windsors.

Previous monarchs (amazing to relate) had been remarkably slow to perceive the pleasure to be derived from introducing corgis into their lives. George V had, I am told, an ill-tempered parrot, Edward VII fussed over a terrier called Caesar, while Queen Victoria wasted her time with a lap-dog called John Broon.

These dark, corgi-deprived days are happily long past. HRH now seldom stirs unless accompanied by at least half-a-dozen corgis. In this – as in so many other things – she is a shining example to her subjects.

Susan even travelled with the Queen (Princess Elizabeth

as she was then) and Prince Philip on their honeymoon. Some of the tips she picked up during those weeks at Birkhall on the Balmoral estate proved very useful to her soon afterwards.

Within the year she produced her first litter of puppies. And so our dynasty began. Some of us currently in the royal entourage are eleventh or twelfth generation descendants of that first happy union between Susan and the dashingly named Rozavel Lucky Strike.

By and large the strain has been kept pure. Some mindless hunk of prime championship-winning corgi is hand-picked to father each new generation of the line. It helps keep us healthy, happy and sane.

'We should have done something similar with the children,' the Duke of Edinburgh remarked over breakfast only the other day, when the topic was being discussed.

There is, it has to be admitted, one blot upon our escutcheon. And, I'm afraid, Princess Margaret is responsible for it. She should have kept her bumptious little long-haired-dachshund, Pipkin, under closer control.

But these things happen. And the result of this thing happening was a 'dorgi'. The dorgi is a curious hybrid which is to be admired in so far as it resembles a corgi and pitied in so far as it looks like a long-haired dachshund that has been raised by Princess Margaret.

We have two dorgis in the royal entourage at the moment, Harris and his nephew Brandy. I try, of course, to treat them as equals, to include them in our games and sports. But it is hard. They are not like us. For one thing they keep mumbling about 'badgers' in heavily accented German.

Apart from myself, there are six corgis currently in the Royal Household. Pride of place goes to Kelpie, who keeps a close eye on her daughter Phoenix and her grand-daughter Pharos. Then there are the sisters Flora and Swift, and the incorrigible Fib.

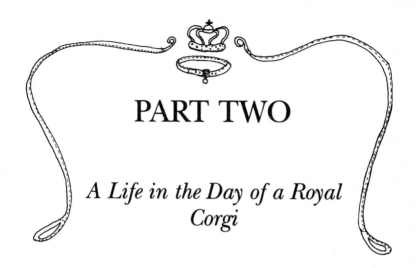

PART TWO

A Life in the Day of a Royal Corgi

Informal yet decorous

A t Buckingham Palace I, together with all the other Royal Corgis – and the two Royal Dorgis – sleep in a specially converted box room just down the corridor from the Queen's own bedroom suite. It is a well-appointed room on the first floor.

It is furnished – unlike most of the Palace – with an eye for comfort rather than show. Wicker baskets, old cushions and canvas-covered chairs are scattered with careless profusion. The result is (I consider) very successful: informal yet decorous.

The room, moreover, has that delightful sweet-yet-savoury scent that can only be achieved by cramming half a dozen dogs into a small windowless space for long periods of time.

Generally we rise at seven-thirty. A royal footman comes in and announces that breakfast is served. We scramble out into the corridor and discover our bowls laid out on an attractive strip of green plastic sheeting. I sometimes hear it said by common and ignorant mongrels that we dine off solid silver plate and eat nothing but prime steak. This is not true. We favour plastic bowls (they are softer on the nose) and a wholesome mixture of tinned meat and dog-biscuits.

Soon after eight we proceed down the King's Corridor and present ourselves to HRH. She is usually in her study casting an eye over her Red Boxes – or the *Daily Telegraph* crossword. We greet each other effusively. Although famously strict about matters of decorum, we are prepared to waive our rules when dealing with the Queen.

We follow the Queen through to her breakfast. On a good day one can expect to get a finger of toast spread with butter, and perhaps even a bit of bacon. Occasionally, the Duke of Edinburgh is present too, but this has little effect on the fare available. He contents himself with a disgusting-looking mixture of yoghurt, bran and dried fruit; it is not the sort of dish that can be easily offered to a corgi, nor is it the sort of dish a corgi would want to eat.

Throughout the royal breakfast the Queen's pipe-major, stationed under the breakfast-room window, plays a selection of Scottish airs. Some people, I am told, find the noise of the bagpipes unpleasant, but to my ears it is delightful: it sounds like a cat being strangled.

For our morning walk the Queen might take us out into the gardens to feed the ducks. There are thirty-nine acres of garden surrounding the Palace; it is a perfect romping ground for corgis. And at the centre of the garden is the lake, busy with ducks, geese, swans and even flamingos.

The Queen stands at the water's edge in her galoshes regally distributing the specially cut cubes of stale bread to the grateful birds, while the corgis form a guard of honour round her, ready to repulse the advance of any over-eager goose or swan. Life as a Royal Corgi has its responsibilities.

Although most of the birds are fed on stale bread, the flamingos are given shrimps. Prince Philip says that they need their special diet in order to maintain their pink colour, but this theory is clearly incorrect. The other morning Fib managed to purloin the packet of shrimps intended for the flamingos. He ate the lot. But we are still waiting for him to turn even faintly pink. So much for the Duke of Edinburgh's knowledge of Wildlife.

Most weeks the Queen hosts a small informal lunch-party at the Palace for a motley collection of 'high-achievers'. We, and the Queen, wait for them all to assemble in one of the drawing-rooms and then – moving in close formation – we sweep in amongst them.

It is hard to work out how the Queen chooses her guest

list. Many of the people she invites seem almost unable to speak. When she approaches them they just stand before her mouthing noiselessly (which is bad) or babbling incomprehensively (which is worse). Nearly all of them hop from one foot to the other in a sort of dance of welcome. It is not a pretty sight. But the Queen, ever the perfect hostess, refrains from remarking upon it.

Soon after one we all go through to the dining-room. While the guests find their seats, we take up our stations under the table around the Queen's chair. Our special duty is to protect and defend the Queen's unofficial regalia – her handbag. The Royal Handbag – during meal-times – is hung from a discreet hook under the dining-room table where we are able to keep a close watch on it.

The Queen, always grateful for our unstinting vigilance, rewards us regularly throughout the meal with broken

The dance of welcome

breadsticks. Many of the ignorant guests assume that we are sitting under the table merely hoping to be fed with fragments of *grissini*. Little do they realise the true purpose of our presence.

(Although one does not wish to tempt the Fates by boasting, it has to be said that – thus far – we have an enviable record of success. While most other areas of royal security have been found wanting, our defences have never been breached: no one has been able to snatch the Queen's handbag.)

At three the Queen rises from the table and the guests depart. We can relax again. After we have seen the last visitor off the premises, we go for another stroll round the grounds. We might watch the Duke of Edinburgh taking off in his red Wessex helicopter from the Palace heli-pad, or Prince Edward playing tennis on the Palace courts, or we

Our special duty

might make an inspection tour of the royal stables.

In the evening we will sit with the Queen in her private sitting-room while she finishes her work (or her *Daily Telegraph* crossword). Perhaps we might even watch television with her. She is very fond of programmes about horses – *The Horse of the Year Show, Only Fools and Horses, Channel 4 Racing* etc. But I am sure this is only because there aren't any programmes about corgis.

After supper, if it is a pleasant evening, we might accompany the Queen (and a royal footman) for a last turn around the garden. We are obliged to bark a great deal on these nocturnal excursions so that the guards know we are coming and don't inadvertently shoot us (or – worse still – ignore us completely).

And then it's home to bed. There is a royal detective who sleeps outside our room on a sofa. He doesn't wear shoes, so as not to wake us unnecessarily, but he has strict instructions to rouse us if there is any threat to the Royal Handbag.

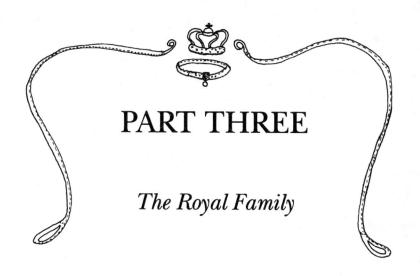

PART THREE

The Royal Family

A memorable occasion

❧ *The Queen* ❧

The Queen is a remarkable woman. People often go on about her innate sense of majesty or her imposing presence. And this is certainly one of the faces that she presents to the world. But, for myself, I have to say that I have always found her warm-hearted, sympathetic and fun-loving.

She is an ideal dog-lover, being only a little over five-foot tall (or short). It is no trouble at all for her to bend down and scratch our heads or tickle our stomachs. She understands, moreover, the great trinity of a corgi's existence: regular snacks, regular walks, and regular evenings spent curled up on the sofa (indeed it is not so very different from her own regime).

The other corgis and I are enormously fond of her. The stories I have heard circulating that we actually bite her are, I assure you, nothing but wicked rumours put about by jealous courtiers.

We love her. We would protect her – and her handbag – with our lives.

❧ *The Duke of Edinburgh* ❧

Prince Philip is an alarming presence about the Palace. One has to be careful not to get under his feet. He marches about dressed in his full naval uniform – or in nothing but a bath towel – giving orders to the servants, his family and, indeed, us.

At least we can understand what he is going on about, which is more than can be said for his family or the servants. He speaks our language: he barks.

It is not, however, a particular comfort to be able to understand what he is saying. He holds, for example, alarming views about the necessity of culling animal populations in order to improve their stock. And he seems to take particular delight in discoursing upon these matters in our hearing – often when he is cleaning his gun. There is a glint in his eye that quite frightens poor Fib. It makes me uneasy too.

Outside he is even more dangerous. Although he has a black taxi and a red helicopter he doesn't really approve of motorised transport. He prefers to drive around in a coach

A cause of uneasiness

and four with a tartan rug over his knees. The contraption is seldom under control and the wheels seem positively designed to crush corgis.

Prince Philip's quarters have none of the comforts that make the Queen's so pleasant. There are no capacious armchairs or low sofas for corgis to rest in. Everything is decidedly spartan. The only animal companion he seems to tolerate is the mouse that he keeps tethered to his new computer.

⚜ Prince Charles ⚜

The Prince of Wales is a generous and serious-minded spirit, ever eager to help others. Despite his hectic schedule and numerous cares, he is always solicitous for our well-being. When staying at the Palace, or at one of the Royal residences, he will frequently interrupt his duties and insist on taking us out for a walk.

He cannot, however, escape his commitments for long, and often – even on these brief strolls to the bottom of the garden – he is obliged to bring his mobile phone along.

He is in frequent contact with various spiritual advisors. His two key mentors in metaphysical matters are Sir Laurens van der Post and Camilla Parker Bowles. With the former he discusses his role in this world, with the latter he mulls over his hopes and fears for the next life – the mysteries of reincarnation and the transmigration of souls.

Above all things Charles is a communicator. He has a restless desire to share his thoughts and opinions. It is, I am sure, one of the reasons he is seldom without his mobile phone. But he does not confine himself to talking to humans. He talks to corgis, he talks to flowers, he even talks to cabbages.

On one memorable occasion he persuaded Mrs Parker Bowles to come and talk to some cabbages with him. Cabbages, like many vegetables, are however notoriously hard of hearing, and the royal nature-lover and his friend were obliged actually to lie down in the cabbage patch in order to make themselves heard. What a touching and comical sight it was – certainly very much more amusing than the Prince's *Goon Show* impersonations.

Although Prince Charles is always considerate towards us, it has to be admitted against him that he, himself, does not possess a corgi. He did have an irritating little terrier called Pooh, that would follow him about yapping excitedly and bolting down rabbit holes.

There is no need to dwell on Pooh's sudden disappearance (and certainly nothing was ever proved against Fib), but Prince Charles seemed to make an unaccountable fuss about the incident. After all Pooh was only a terrier.

Despite the trauma of loss, Prince Charles soon replaced Pooh with another faithful hound. This one was called Dimbleby, and had the virtue of not bolting down rabbit holes.

Even so, to make sure that he did not lose this new canine companion, Charles had Dimbleby followed at all times by a whole crew of people with cameras, lights and tape-recorders. It seemed to be overdoing it rather. And, moreover, the measure wasn't particularly effective: recently Dimbleby too has disappeared. I have questioned Fib closely but he protests his innocence. So the matter remains a mystery. And Charles remains, for the moment, without a pet dog.

Charles's generosity is famous. Recently he has taken to carrying about small packets of plain oaten biscuits and he distributes these goodies liberally amongst us. They are delicious. 'You seem to be the only ones who really appreciate them,' he remarked (a touch sadly, I thought) the other day. It is a wonder to me that other breeds don't enjoy these snacks, as they seem to me the ideal dog-biscuit: thick, dry and savourless. Corgis, however, are often ahead of the times. Where we lead others will follow.

❧ *Princess Diana* ❧

When Diana was first introduced to us back in 1981 she made a very agreeable impression. Although I do recall there was a lingering odour of pre-school children about her clothes which we all found slightly disconcerting. When she became Princess of Wales soon afterwards, however, we were inclined to overlook even this. She was now, after all, Welsh. And we Welsh stick together. Besides she seemed such a nice girl.

Her habit of feeding us under the table at dinner with tid-bits from her own plate was very much appreciated. Indeed, such was her generosity that she would frequently give us almost her entire meal. And in return for these little kindnesses we would let her stroke us without snapping at her fingers. A corgi can do no more.

She seemed genuinely fond of us. Imitation is, they say, the sincerest form of flattery, and we were touched to note how she started imitating our special 'pleading' look: head cocked to one side, eyes dewy with unspoken longing, a pathetic whine issuing between trembling lips. It is a highly successful way of eliciting sympathy and getting what you want. Corgis have been employing it for generations as a means of getting chocolate drops.

What Diana wanted it for we couldn't fathom, as she didn't like chocolate. Indeed, it seemed to disagree with her. Not that she didn't try hard to develop a taste for it. Often she would gamely eat her way through several bars of the

Poor Kelpie was badly startled

stuff. But invariably it would make her sick as a cat. Poor thing.

Diana's real fault, however, in our opinion was her clumsiness. Whether it was caused by her habit of wearing dark glasses indoors, or that she simply didn't look where she was going, remains open to debate. But she was always tripping over us.

This was undignified. It was not commensurate with our royal position. It was dangerous, alarming and noisy. And I don't suppose it was very much better for Diana.

One morning at Sandringham, when she was walking along the passageway with her head in the air (or perhaps it was buried in a copy of the *Daily Mail*), she tripped over Kelpie who was lying, as she has been accustomed to lie for many years, at the top of the main staircase. Poor Kelpie was badly startled, while Diana for her part crashed loudly down the flight of stairs.

One regrets to relate that she showed not the least concern for the hapless Kelpie. Indeed, with an unattractive – though not untypical – selfishness she lay groaning on the hall floor, making such a pitiful sound that *everyone* ignored poor Kelpie.

Moreover, the banister (a beautiful piece of hand-turned oak) was severely splintered by Diana's high-heeled shoe during her descent. But did she have the good grace to admit to this? Alas, not. And in the absence of the true explanation Prince Philip very ungallantly put it about that the damage had been done by 'the corgis scratching at the woodwork'.

On another occasion Diana tumbled over Phoenix and crashed straight through a valuable glass-fronted display cabinet. Phoenix was showered with broken glass and was lucky to escape without serious injury. Even so, for several days afterwards we had to tread carefully over the carpets, keeping an eye out for the glass shards.

We don't see Diana very often now. It is, one suspects, fear of further breakages that has persuaded the Queen to curtail her visits. HRH has so many valuable and beautiful ornaments about the Palace (not least ourselves) that it is simply too dangerous to have Diana in the place.

꙳   *Wills and Harry*   ꙳

It is sometimes said that corgis don't like children. Nothing could be further from the truth: we love children. They are delicious – tender, defenceless, and tasty. They tend to wear shorts which gives us a clear view of their biteable little legs. It is only when they grow up that they become more problematic.

Alas, both the young royal princes have now got beyond the age when they can be bitten with impunity. William, although the elder, remains the easier prey of the two. He has such good manners that he is reluctant to kick and, besides, he is often in a daze after one of those many blows to the head that he receives at his progressive prep school.

Harry is a more difficult proposition. With his shaggy red hair and impish grin I sometimes mistake him for a fellow corgi. Under this disguise he is able to catch us unawares. He has, I am afraid to say, been known to pull our tails.

⚜ *Princess Anne* ⚜

The Princess Royal's arrivals at Buckingham Palace are like sharp blasts of country air. She strides through the Palace

Save Corgis from the Children

24

portals, bringing in her wake a cloud of country smells – horses, wet dogs, wet husbands and teenage children.

Her language can be a trifle fierce, but even it is not as alarming as Eglantyne, her bull terrier. I had understood that Mr Major had passed some sort of law against bull terriers (it seemed to be another happy example of his general concern for corgis), but the legislation does not appear to be biting. The same, alas, cannot be said for Eglantyne, who takes any and every opportunity to sink her teeth in living flesh. Princess Anne is quite unconcerned by her bull terrier's antics. Despite the Queen's protests, she just laughs as Eglantyne chases us round the house.

The Princess's children are every bit as rowdy as her dog (and their names are almost as strange). And yet the Princess is apparently the head of a group called 'Save the Children'. It seems to me that 'Save Corgis from the Children' would be a more useful and fitting organisation.

The only soothing element in the Princess's household is provided by the mysterious man who follows her about. He is a nondescript fellow, silent, stiff-backed, weak-chinned, low-browed, with a name like Mark, or Tim or Philip or something. His purpose is not readily apparent, but I suppose he is some sort of factotum.

❧   *Prince Andrew*   ❧

Andrew is certainly the noisiest of the Queen's children. Even now he still races around the Palace corridors doing aeroplane impressions, rugby-tackling unwary visitors, shouting 'Hello Sailor', or wielding his new golf clubs.

He is a man of enthusiasm. We all remember his passion for photography a few years back. He would dash about taking snaps of everything: the garden, the horse guards,

A fresh danger

the Duke of Edinburgh, and – of course – us. He even produced a book of these pictures which Prince Philip – ever the proud father – used as a mat for his coffee cup.

At another moment Andrew toyed with the idea of taking up painting. Rather than working in water-colour like his older brother, he decided to experiment with more radical materials. For his effort he painted a group of photographers with a red paint-spray-gun. The effect was certainly exciting – but I'm not sure whether it was Art.

He decided, however, against pursuing this interest, and recently has turned instead to golf. This has added a fresh danger to Palace life. It is not safe now to walk along the upper corridors; the sound of crashing vases is deafening, and poor Swift has been struck several times by misdirected putts.

Another of Andrew's noisy and dangerous hobbies of recent years has been Fergie.

❧ *Fergie* ❧

We were delighted when Fergie first came to live at the Palace. We all thought we were going to get on well with her. After all she had corgi colouring. And she was down on our level for much of the time. Her habit of rolling about laughing on the carpet at all times of the day and night (even when conferring with her financial advisors) was both fun and infectious.

There seemed to be an instinctive generosity about her. The word 'Hello' was forever on her lips. She was always eager to provide succour (I think that is the term) for celebrity guests and misplaced Americans anxious about their hair-loss.

It was only after a while that we realised she was stealing our food. Not our special 'By Royal Appointment' Pedigree Chum – (Liver and Tripe Supreme) – although Swift always insists that she was at this too. But our chocolate drops, and the cuts of cold beef and lamb that were often left over after Sunday lunch and usually found their way into our bowls for Monday breakfast. We could sometimes catch the greedy Duchess sneaking into the Palace larders and carrying off these trophies to her room.

This, I suppose, was just another of the Duchess's special diets. One afternoon it would be exotic fruits, and by the evening it would be our chocolate drops.

Another reason for the late-night kitchen raids was that Fergie often returned to the Palace, after a night on the town, so late that all the kitchen staff had gone to bed. She and her fellow revellers – usually an uncouth Scot and his excitable wife – would then go crashing about the backstairs corridors, roaring for food, drink, Kaliber, or exotic fruits (depending on what the diet of the moment was).

During the years of Fergie's residence at the Palace it was

rare for us to get an uninterrupted night's sleep. When Prince Andrew was at home she would be shouting at him; when he was away on Naval duty she would be shouting at her friends; when she herself was away on ski-ing duty, the two little princesses would be shouting just for the hell of it. The Palace was not a restful place in those days.

We were shocked, moreover, by Fergie's lack of sensitivity – by her disloyalty even. Instead of telling the two little princesses stories about corgis and queens (such as any young girl would love to hear) she would bore on, every bedtime, about a budgerigar called 'Helicopter'.

In a crude way, I suppose, the stories were effective: Beatrice and Eugenie would nod off almost immediately. Indeed they would sometimes even feign sleep as soon as Fergie suggested telling one of these 'Helicopter' tales.

Nevertheless, the whole notion of budgerigars seemed to me and the other corgis so suburban, so vulgar. Many of the courtiers thought so too.

Now that Fergie has moved out of the Palace (and gone to live – I hear – in a blue plastic pyramid) things are very much quieter, and sleeping dogs can get some sleep.

❧ *Prince Edward* ❧

Edward is the prince that we see most of. He still lives in the Palace full-time. His tidy, poster-bedecked room has changed little over the years.

Although he is a serious-minded young fellow he is not averse to socialising. When he has friends over, he will often stay up quite late showing off his Michael Ball CD collection or his prowess with an electric kettle and a tea-bag.

Amongst the ardent admirers from the world of show business who call on the Prince, one sometimes glimpses the mysterious figure known as Andrew Lloyd Webber or the 'Phantom of the Musical'.

It is said that this man is so terrifying to look at that he spends most of his days in the bowels of a London theatre composing music upon a vast organ. Reputedly he wears a mask to conceal his face, but I have seen this so-called mask and it is, I assure you, quite as terrifying as whatever might lie underneath it.

Prince Edward's enthusiasm for showbiz manifested itself early – much to the horror of his parents. He even had the audacity to try and train me and the other dogs up into a performing troupe. There are, however, some things that a Royal Corgi will not do. Dignity does have to be maintained. Protocol must be observed. The very idea of us all dressed in ridiculous costumes leaping through hoops or balancing things on our noses!

In the end he had to admit defeat. And, instead, he got his siblings to perform these degrading tricks. They had to wear the silly outfits and prance through the coloured hoops. 'It's a Royal Knockout', the young Prince kept shouting excitedly. And I must say, I rather agreed with him.

⚜ *The Queen Mother* ⚜

For many years the Queen Mother has been a consoling presence on the royal scene: a vision in duck-egg blue, trailed by the gentle scent of juniper berries.

She, of course, has a special place in the hearts of all corgis as the person who first introduced us into the Royal Household. She still has a couple of corgis of her own, and our trips over to Clarence House to visit these royal cousins are always happy occasions.

The Queen Mother understands the importance of eating

well. She is very generous with the chocolate drops, and very careful not to give us any dangerous fish-bones in the lunch-time scraps.

The Queen Mother's love of animals extends beyond corgis to embrace horses. She is always keeping an eye on her horses on the television. Many an afternoon is passed with her perched happily on the sofa watching the gee-gees, a glass of champagne in one hand, the telephone in the other. She is in constant touch with her friend Mr William Hill, discussing the finer points of the horses and pledging large sums of money towards their upkeep and well-being.

❧ *Princess Michael of Kent* ❧

One thing to remember about the Royal Family is that it *is* a family. In other words, it is overburdened with relations (i.e. people one doesn't particularly care for but can't possibly get rid of). These 'relations' are forever turning up for a free dinner or a swim in the Palace pool. The Queen is perfectly polite to them all but I must say that I and my fellow corgis find it a remarkable strain.

Princess Michael (an odd name for a Princess I always think) is a regular visitor, often popping in to use the Palace photocopier. She is Austrian – or is it Australian, or perhaps it's both? Certainly, she has none of that innate British love of dogs.

In fact, I think she has cats. She always smells distinctly Siamese (an awful aroma, as anyone with a sensitive nose will know). Very sensibly she tries to mask it with virulent perfume. And sometimes she even tries to disguise herself completely by donning a red wig. But she can't deceive a corgi's sense of smell.

The merest whiff of cat is enough to set us off. We always

start up a terrific din of barking as soon as she comes through the door. I am not sure that the Princess doesn't enjoy all the attention. She whirls about in our midst, performing some sort of Austrian (or, perhaps, Australian) folk dance, whooping excitedly, while the Queen stands clapping her hands and shouting general encouragement.

Unfortunately the Princess can be rather over-vigorous, and more than once she has caught poor Flora with the diamond-tipped point of her high-heeled shoe. But these little things happen when you are having fun.

The Princess is often accompanied by a silent man in a beard. I have never caught his name. He doesn't join in the romps but stands silently to one side with his hands clasped in front of him – or sometimes, for variety, behind him.

⚜ *Viscount Linley* ⚜

We always enjoy the too-rare visits of Viscount Linley to the Palace. His presence at meals usually ensures rich pickings for us corgis, as he is quite likely to pick up a bread roll and hurl it at Prince Edward's head with a shout of 'I'm not a Hooray Henry! Hooray!' In no time at all the dining-room carpet is strewn with rolls, butter-pats, After Eights and other delights.

The Viscount has, I understand, made quite a name for himself in his carpentry business with his special line of collapsable furniture. Certainly the side-table he made for the Queen is always collapsing most efficiently.

❦ *Princess Margaret* ❧

Linley's mother (and the Queen's sister) is of a rather different stamp, although in her own way she is quite prone to collapsing. I think she is often thrown off balance by the huge glass of water (and whisky) that she carries with her at all times.

But while her son is thoughtfully tossing bread rolls about for our benefit, all that one can hope for from Princess Margaret is a scattering of cigarette ash. As she is not much taller than a full grown corgi, there is very little time to dodge these showers.

Nothing is more irritating to a well turned out corgi than to have his recently groomed coat besmirched with fag ash. More than once I have felt obliged to nip the Princess's

Nothing more irritating . . .

ankle by way of reprimand. She does not, however, seem to pay any attention to such hints.

❧ *Major Ron* ❧

Of all the extended Royal Family the member who provides the greatest pleasure and the most intoxicating fun is the Duchess of York's delightful father, Ronald 'Major Ron' Ferguson. The laughs, the japes, the games we have on his visits to the Royal Household!

He is a man who enjoys rolling on the floor (his daughter takes after him in this respect). And he is a man capable of persuading others to roll on the floor with him. Of course corgis delight in this sort of frolicking. I have spent many a happy afternoon dancing about the prostrate form of Major Ron yapping with pleasure and excitement.

The Major has that gift of making himself at home anywhere. While others are often intimidated by the formal air of the Palace he is very much at his ease, rocking back on his chair and giving friendly advice to the Duke of Edinburgh on where to 'relax' in central London.

The Duke is always thrown in to a state of amazement by Major Ron's breadth of knowledge of this and other subjects. Indeed, quite often, after the Major's departure, he will remark in a tone of blank bewilderment to no one in particular, 'I really can't believe that man.'

The Major, despite his fabled sporting prowess on the polo field and at the Wigmore Club, is also a keen amateur of the decorative arts. On several occasions I have noticed him surreptitiously admiring the royal coffee spoons – marvellous pieces of Georgian silver.

It is a great sadness that in recent years we have seen so much less of the 'Galloping Major'. I understand that (like myself) he has been engaged in writing his memoirs. I know that this does take up a great deal of time but I do think he might make the effort to visit occasionally.

The Queen feels his absence keenly, I know. One evening when we were watching some television chat show together, who should bounce on to the screen but the good Major. At the sight of the familiar tufted eyebrows the Queen let out a short gasp and rocking forward on the sofa, began to weep. 'I can't bear it,' she sobbed. She misses him terribly – just as we do.

It was all too much for her, and she quickly flicked over to *LA Law*.

PART FOUR

One's Home Comforts

A magnificent building

❧ *Buckingham Palace* ❧

Of our several homes Buckingham Palace is perhaps the favourite. It is a magnificent building with acres of carpeted corridors inside and acres of well-kept garden outside.

Unsurprisingly, it is very popular with visitors. Many is the morning one can expect to see a party of German tourists scrambling over the garden wall for a look round the grounds or even an eager royal-watcher slipping through a half-open window in the hope of sharing a quiet matutinal cigarette with the Queen.

Or perhaps there will be an American visitor dropping in around eleven, full of the excitements of hang-gliding. (Unfortunately, Americans seem to have little under-standing of the unspoken dress-code that prevails at the Palace and sometimes arrive without their trousers.)

Although the Queen does like to preserve a degree of informality in her dealings with the public, there are limits. And it was thought, as the number of unscheduled visitors calling on the Palace increased, that it would be a good idea to formalise matters.

As a result HRH has recently introduced guided tours. Visitors are now expected to present themselves at the side entrance and pay a modest £8.50 entry fee. This seems to be a remarkably satisfactory solution to the problem.

Alas, the pressure of numbers does mean that some of the more personal touches of the old system have had to be abandoned. It was not thought to be possible for *every* member of the visiting public to traipse into the Queen's bedroom for a cigarette and a whinge about the state of the nation. So that item has been dropped from the tour.

Nevertheless, despite such restrictions, the popularity of Buckingham Palace remains undiminished. Indeed, some visitors are so eager to get a look at this great royal residence that they still can't wait for the gates to open.

❧ *Windsor Castle* ❧

Windsor is essentially our weekend home; it is close to London and it offers some diverting pastimes. One can chase ramblers in the Park, and there is always the chance to nip a young Etonian out in the town.

Much of the actual Castle, however, is horribly old-fashioned and incommodious, and many of the furnishings are quite dreadful. The Queen had taken some of these matters in hand and had launched a plan of refurbishment, but we corgis felt that the scheme did not go nearly far enough. The chintz curtains in the dining-room, for example, were scheduled to remain. That, of course, was before Fib took matters into his own paws and nudged the offending drapes into the flame of a building-contractor's gas-heater.

In no time at all the curtains had been entirely consumed by fire, as indeed had the dining-room and much of St George's Chapel. Everything, I am happy to say, is to be replaced with a much lighter, more comfortable and modern scheme.

Nor has this been Fib's only contribution to the new-look Windsor that is rapidly springing into being. For some time now the head gardener has been complaining about Fib's habit of burying bones in the Castle grounds.

Took matters into his own paws

In an effort to discover where Fib has concealed all his trophies, there has recently been a major initiative with workmen digging up much of the Park and sinking great shafts into the ground.

They are obviously very pleased with their progress, as the scheme seems to be continuing and growing. Meanwhile Fib, demoralised at losing so many of his bones to these drillers, has taken to hiding any new bones he gets under the cushions on the sofa.

⚜ *Balmoral* ⚜

The annual excursions to Balmoral are always a treat. The long walks in the rain (if not snow) are full of excitement:

the scent of rabbits, foxes, stoats, wild-cats and press photographers are forever titillating our nostrils and sending us scampering off into the rhododendrons.

The house itself is not as warm as it might be, and the vast expanses of tartan carpeting are positively disconcerting to a small dog. Nevertheless all those mad checks of colour do serve some useful purpose. They conceal stains wonderfully well.

If it is too wet or too cold to go outside with comfort (and it often is), one can avail oneself of the indoor facilities, safe in the knowledge that no one (i.e. the Duke of Edinburgh) is going to discover it until well after the event, if at all.

The other tartan aspect of life at Balmoral is less satisfactory. With most of the male members of the family wearing kilts, one has to remember to keep one's eyes fixed firmly on the ground at all times. To look up would be too

Too alarming . . .

alarming.

Some people, however, have very peculiar interests. Fib was actually approached by a French magazine that wanted him to smuggle a camera into the ballroom at Balmoral and take a picture of Prince Charles from this unflattering angle. Fib, however, who is deeply suspicious of anybody who isn't (at least partly) Welsh, refused to co-operate.

Sight, moreover, is not the only sense that can be offended up at Balmoral. The family habit of singing round the grand piano in the evening often produces sounds uncomfortably redolent of cats courting on the rooftops. It is always enough to send Flora off into a frenzy of barking; she is such a sensitive creature.

❧ *Sandringham* ❧

If Balmoral is cold and wet, Sandringham manages to be cold even without the wetness. It is always freezing there. A wind blows down off the Arctic tundra across the Norfolk Broads and straight under the doors. For this reason it is always advisable to find a seat on a chair or sofa. The floor is too draughty for comfortable snoozing.

Despite the constant chill factor, one is expected to go outside and race around giving encouragement to people with guns – as if shooting was any proper way to kill birds.

We corgis know that it is far better sport to rush upon them and bite their necks before they even leave the ground. But the Duke of Edinburgh seems strangely inflexible when it comes to death-dealing, and insists on sticking to his shot-guns.

PART FIVE

The Staff

A rare event

❧ *Courtiers* ❧

The Palace is, of course, crawling with courtiers, simpering gentlemen with fixed smiles and permanent stoops.

They are horribly jealous of us corgis, as they recognise that we are the Queen's closest confidants and companions. And, given half a chance, they will try to administer a swift kick with their patent-leather court shoes. These, in fact, are little more than slippers and are no good for kicking, so we have the advantage of them there, too.

As a result, they leave us alone a good deal and content themselves with wandering about muttering little mantras, such as, 'Fergie, Fergie, Fergie; Vulgar, Vulgar, Vulgar', in an effort to keep calm. Or they console themselves by talking to nice sympathetic girls from the *Spectator*.

❧ *Servants* ❧

The servants are scarcely better than the courtiers, although they console *themselves* by talking, not to nice sympathetic girls from the *Spectator*, but to nice sympathetic men from the *News of the World*.

For the most part, however, they are idle gossips. It is not often that we are menaced by a vacuum cleaner on the stairs, or have our noses disturbed by over-vigorous dusting.

A few of the staff members, it is true, do have interests and hobbies of their own. Some Palace servants hold regular nude wrestling bouts in their own quarters in the Royal Mews. Prince Charles's valet – before his premature retirement – was an enthusiastic amateur photographer (an interest picked up from Prince Andrew perhaps), while another of his servants has, I understand, a keen interest in commemorative cuff-links.

Princess Anne's staff is not without its hobbyists either. One of her servants displayed a precocious interest in the niceties of epistolary style and was forever rootling through her red letter-cases in search of fine examples of the letter-writer's art.

The Royal Family, however, has never held literary accomplishments in high regard. And this studious servant, perhaps feeling uncomfortable in the uncultured atmosphere of the Palace, soon left.

❧ *The Palace Postman* ❧

One thing royal corgis have in common with all lesser dogs is the pleasure of chasing the postman each morning. The Queen, it has to be said, has her own personal postie – the Royal Messenger. So at least we know who we are biting. And, of course, he knows who is biting him. This seems a much more satisfactory arrangement than the one endured by the general run of dogs.

From my conversations with my less fortunate fellows I understand that many dogs have to make to with a wide variety of different postmen. This, of course, can give them the advantage of surprise in their ambushes, but it does mean they don't know who or what they are sinking their teeth into. And where it might have been. Besides, although it may seem old-fashioned to say it, the whole notion of the

A satisfactory arrangement

surprise attack seems somehow unsporting.

In our daily duels with the Royal Messenger there is an undercurrent of mutual respect. He knows that we are waiting for him. We know that he is coming.

He travels (and this is another advantage he has over the conventional postman) in a horse-drawn carriage. This gives plenty of opportunity for barking at the wheels and frightening the horses. (Motor transport, although many dogs will dispute the fact, seems peculiarly unsusceptible to barking).

The Press Corps

One of the less agreeable features of royal life is the almost constant – though happily distant – presence of a group of sad and evil-smelling misfits. These unofficial courtiers are known collectively as the 'Press Corpse'.

The name is obscure, although as a group they are always *pressing* forward, desperate to catch some word or signal, from the royal entourage as it sweeps past. And they smell, moreover, distinctly like a three-day-old corpse that has been steeped in embalming fluid. This embalming-fluid aroma, although discernable first thing in the morning, is, I have noticed, always more pronounced after lunch.

Bobo

Until very recently the key servant, as everyone at the Palace knew, was the Queen's 'number one' dresser, Margaret MacDonald – or Bobo. Sadly, she passed away last year and they have had to replace her with four or five lesser figures. Bobo had looked after the Queen since she was a small girl. (Since the Queen was a small girl that is, not Bobo. It is hard to believe that Bobo was ever anything other than a quietly formidable old woman.) She guarded the Queen jealously. She was always the first person to see her each morning. It was she who decided which pastel-shaded outfit HRH would wear for the day.

Of all the royal servants she was the only one whose relationship with the Queen in any way approached our own. Ours, however (as anyone with any familiarity with the Royal Household would readily acknowledge), is really much the closer and stronger.

Bobo, for example, was never encouraged to curl up on HRH's lap while watching *Rumpole of the Bailey*. Nor did she ever spend whole afternoons playing with the Queen on the lawn at Balmoral.

Perhaps inevitably Miss MacDonald came to resent our privileged position. As a Scot, moreover, she found it difficult to accept that the Queen should ever favour a Welsh breed of dog.

She was forever attempting to press the rival claims of such ridiculous canine types as the Dandy Dinmont and the West Highland Terrier. Perfectly useful dogs I'm sure, if you want to catch rabbits or chase wild haggises over the moors, but they would be no good at a Garden Party. They lack the sociable herding instincts of us corgis. And, besides, all Scottish dogs are notoriously mean.

Despite these tensions we were always studiously polite to Bobo in public. Petty jealousies are one of the inescapable features of court life, and we do our best to rise above them.

PART SIX

Visitors

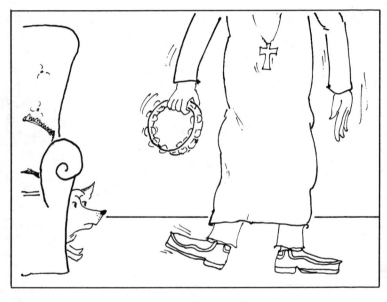

Not seen – or heard – it again

❧ *The Archbishop of Canterbury* ❧

Time was when the Archbishops of Canterbury were quiet unassuming men, responsible for spreading tranquillity and peace. We all remember the last one, Dr Runcie, very fondly. He would often soothe us, and the Queen, to sleep (even in the cold and uncomfortable chapel at Windsor) with his gently cooing tones. That particular sing-song lilt he had perfected was wonderfully good at inducing sleep.

The same, alas, cannot be said of this new fellow, Carey. His visits are always times of considerable alarm at the Palace. As he clumps about noisily in his inaptly named Hush-puppies, we run for cover. Even when he has settled down to tea one is not safe. He won't sit still for a moment, but is forever leaping up (spraying tea and cake crumbs in all directions) to punctuate his conversation with cries of 'Halleluliah!', 'Praise Be!' or 'One–Nil to the Arsenal'.

On one occasion he had the temerity to bring a tambourine with him. It did not go down well. Prince Philip remarked that it made him look like a gypsy. So, thank goodness, we haven't seen – or heard – it again.

The Archbishop's attempts at small talk appear to bore the Royal Family. The other day, while he was happily discoursing upon the sacred ties of Holy Matrimony, Prince Charles wandered out of the room. Andrew pretended he had lost a cuff-link down the back of the sofa, the Duke started whistling the *Dam-Busters* theme, and the Queen rather brusquely changed the subject.

❧ *The Prime Minister* ❧

Another regular visitor to the Palace is Mr Major, the PM. He is a sweet, unassuming man. Sometimes I am barely aware of his approach as he creeps silently down the corridor in his grey slip-on shoes.

He seems to feel that he has a particular affinity with us corgis. Often as he heads towards the weekly Tuesday-evening audience with the Queen – between the frequent pauses, U-turns and abrupt halts – he'll take time to stop and pat my head, remarking with an odd rueful air, that he too is in the dog house again.

It is flattering that he regards the Palace as *our* house but it belongs, of course, to the Queen.

I am not sure why Mr Major always looks so rueful. Certainly the previous Prime Minister, Margaret Thatcher – or 'Thatwoman' as the Queen mistakenly called her – never looked rueful. Nor did she ever look where she was going. It was always full speed ahead and woe betide any dog that happened to be lying in her way. She trod on poor Kelpie, who is very deaf and rather slow, on three separate occasions. (She never bothered to learn our names; indeed she referred to Kelpie, on the occasions that she trod on her, as Sir Geoffrey.)

Despite the incidents with Kelpie, it cannot be said that Mrs Thatcher was unconcerned for the deaf generally. Quite the reverse in fact. During *her* weekly audiences she would take care to shout very loudly in case the Queen was going deaf. Happily HRH's hearing is excellent, but Mrs Thatcher's consideration did not go unremarked – at least by the corgis.

The Queen obviously found these weekly encounters enormously stimulating and would often retire to her bed afterwards with a stiff drink in her hand and a hot towel over her head, in order to mull over all the interesting topics discussed.

The meetings with Mr Major follow a different course, but are clearly quite as informative. While Mr Major stands by the fireplace explaining the week's events in a quiet even monotone, the Queen sits in her armchair, listening intently, her eyes closed to block out all distractions. Often Mr Major's news is so momentous that HRH (usually so keen to ask questions and make comments) is quite lost for words, and the Prime Minister is obliged to tiptoe quietly from the room, leaving his sovereign to her deep, and silent, deliberations.

❧ *The Privy Council* ❧

One of the great spectacles of Palace life is the swearing-in of the Privy Council. A troop of overweight, balding middle-aged men are ushered into the Throne Room.

The Queen sits at the far end of the room on her dais. At a given signal she bids the first gentleman approach.

The good man staggers forward. In many cases it is uncertain whether he will be able to make it to the throne, even given a clear run. But the course is, in fact, littered with obstacles. There is a series of low, covered stools laid out at intervals. The hapless fellow has to approach each stool, kneel on it, recite an incomprehensible oath, and then move on.

The manoeuvre of kneeling down and getting up proves too much for most. Many an unfortunate chap has lost his balance, slipped and fallen, rolling, on to the carpet – supplementing the required incomprehensible oath with several more (only too comprehensible) ones.

The Queen keeps a very serious expression throughout

the whole performance. But afterwards she has a jolly good laugh.

The other day she told Prince Edward that it was better than a Royal Variety Performance, and suggested that – if he was thinking of branching into comedy production – he should film it. Diana, she added, knew a man who could rig up an ingenious hidden camera to give the whole thing an authentic fly-on-the-wall effect.

❧ Diplomats ❧

It was a sad day (and one, sadly, before my time) when foreign diplomats were told that they no longer had to present themselves at court wearing black silk breeches and stockings.

Tradition tells of the happy times the Palace corgis used to have at diplomatic receptions, scampering amongst the beautifully displayed calves deciding which well-turned leg to sink their teeth into.

Now, however, we have to make do with a forest of nondescript and unrevealing trouser legs. One cannot tell whether they conceal a spindly unpalatable shank (perhaps even a wooden leg), or a prime piece of biteable flesh. And anyway, it is that much more difficult to make a clean bite when one's mouth is half full of black dress trouser.

There is a danger, too, of concealed sock-suspenders to contend with. It is quite easy to crack a tooth on a sock-suspender buckle, especially if one is not expecting to meet it.

That nice Mr Kissinger was right when he said that the world of Diplomacy is not what it once was.

Happy times

❧ 𝒯he 𝒥ncome 𝒯ax 𝒥nspector ❧

A new visitor to the Palace in recent months has been a small nondescript figure in a dark suit. He carries with him a battered and bulging brief-case. At first glance I thought it was our old friend Mr Major. But then I noticed that the man's tie – an arrangement of tiny crests on a dark-blue background – was rather too daring for the PM.

Who could it be? I was at a loss to imagine, until I overheard the head footman announce him as the Income Tax Inspector.

I don't know who invited him to the Palace. Certainly the Queen was not at all pleased to see him. She was polite, of course. (She is always polite.) But under the table I could see her foot tapping up and down impatiently, and she kept saying, 'Yes, yes; I see, I see,' rather brusquely, as the man droned on about 'Capital Gains', 'Peps' and 'Schedule D'.

We corgis are very sensitive to such things. We don't like to feel that dear HRH is being imposed upon. We detected her discomfort and acted immediately.

Phoenix growled ferociously, Pharos started yapping, while I latched on to the Tax Inspector's ankle. The texture of his grey nylon sock quite set my teeth on edge, but I didn't let this deflect me.

The man sprang up with a yelp, upsetting his cup of tea and sending a sheaf of papers swooshing on to the carpet. 'Get this horror off me!' he screamed, before adding in a quieter, but rather strained voice, 'Your Majesty.'

The Queen pretended to be cross with us. And after a while I let go of the man's leg and slunk under a sofa. But as soon as the Tax Inspector had limped out of the room, HRH clapped her hands and fed us all with pieces of cake from the cake-stand.

She singled me out for special praise. 'Oh, you clever, clever thing,' she said, bestowing me a large morsel of almond slice. You can imagine my sense of pride and happiness.

Now all of us are greatly looking forward to the Tax Inspector's next visit. We shall be ready for him.

⚜ *Libel Lawyers* ⚜

The Queen enjoys her daily newspaper. Most mornings, over breakfast, she will attempt the *Telegraph* crossword. Recently, however, she has started having cross words about other papers besides the *Telegraph*.

It is the smaller format papers that seem to annoy her

most. Despite their large print and numerous pictures, she seems quite unable to understand them. Often on opening up one of these tabloid papers she will shake her head and exclaim, 'What do they mean?!' or 'How can they print that?!'

To help answer these difficult questions she rings up her solicitors. They seem to offer a special newspaper-explanation service. A nice man in a pin-stripe suit comes round and looks over the paper with the Queen. Often it transpires that the Queen's confusion has been caused merely by the fact that the story she was reading wasn't true at all.

This is annoying, but it does have its good side, because the tabloid papers run a competition, with huge cash prizes, for people who can spot untrue stories or deliberate mistakes in the papers. It is almost as much fun as the *Telegraph* crossword.

The Queen has recently started entering these exciting tabloid-funded contests. She is, however, usually helped by the man in the pin-stripe suit, and I think that they must have an agreement to share any winnings.

Often they are closeted together for hours, poring over that day's copy of the *Sun,* consulting reference books and filling in forms. When the Queen shouts 'Bingo' we know she is on to a winner.

A little while back she got a cheque for £500,000 for spotting that the *Sun* had inadvertently published her Christmas Message the week *before* Christmas.

❧   *Anthony Blunt*   ❧

The communal memory of the Royal Corgis preserves the image of Sir Anthony Blunt, the Keeper of the Queen's

Pictures. Although he had long since ceased to patrol the Palace corridors by the time I arrived on the scene, he was, by all accounts, a dapper figure in a well cut grey suit. He could be found either dusting the Van Dycks, or the young assistants who so often accompanied him.

He had no very keen interest in corgis (indeed he once tried to kick Kelpie's grandmother Shadow), but he was, apparently, a great expert on French hens – a curious area of interest for such an urbane gentleman.

He was, I often heard it said, always enveloped in a haze of Penhaligon's lily-of-the-valley. It was quite distinct, although it seems that some people were unable to recognise even this well-known aroma.

At some moment in the late 'seventies Sir Anthony retired. Although no one recalls an official announcement, or a big leaving party, it is remembered that the Duke of Edinburgh remarked, rather uncharitably, 'Thank heavens we've got rid of Blunt. I always thought he smelled a bit fishy.'

That the Duke could possibly have mistaken the aroma of lily-of-the-valley for that of fish seems incredible. But then it is often said that the human nose is a very insensitive instrument. This incident certainly seems to confirm that notion.

❧ *Ted Hughes* ❧

We always look forward to the visits of the Poet Laureate, Mr Hughes. He arrives from his country retreat smelling enticingly of dead ferrets and new-born hedgehogs. A whole lexicon of interesting aromas is contained in just one leg of his frayed corduroy trousers.

A lexicon of interesting aromas

He is clearly a man who has steeped himself – perhaps literally – in nature. His knowledge of animal life and lore reveals itself in many of his works, most famously in his extraordinary cycle of poems, *Corgi*.

Although the *Corgi* collection should really be read as a whole, it is, I think, worth giving a flavour of the work.

Corgi at play

> Day dawns.
> Corgi watches.
> His eye turns to the sun. Opaque.
> Man cannot be Dog.
> Corgi watches;

The kitten crosses
                    The courtyard.
Corgi pounces.
The jaw – trapsprung – closes
Fast.
Kill
Corgi.
Gristle and
                    Blood:
                              Kill.

❧ *Sir John Betjeman* ❧

Amongst the Royal Corgis the memory of the previous Poet
Laureate is still held in high regard. Sir John Betjeman
composed several delightful corgi poems – 'The Diary of a
Palace Corgi', 'How to Get On in High Society', 'Kennel
Club Trials'. But perhaps his best was the one he wrote in
memory of Dookie. I quote it here in full as I have been
shocked to discover that it is much less well-known than it
should be.

On the Death of Dookie, the Royal Corgi

Dear old Dookie! Now he's resting
In his kennel in the sky.
Times like these are rather testing:
Dead dogs make one want to cry.

Lively corgi, I recall him
Nipping at my ankle bone

On that very special morning
As I knelt before the throne.

How he made the Palace brighter
With his funny little ways.
Once he ate a Bishop's mitre;
Oh my word, what happy days.

Now, alas, his bark is muzzled.
All around is drear and glum.
Unope'd stands the food once guzzled:
Tins of Pal and cans of Chum.

Royal servant, faithful fellow,
Will we see his like again?
Though the days are turning mellow
We could still be in for rain.

⚜ *Portrait Painters* ⚜

One of the Queen's less agreeable duties is to have to stand
for hours on end (often with her crown on her head) while
her likeness is very slowly captured on a piece of canvas by a
grey-haired man wearing a cravat, or perhaps a succession of
grey-haired men wearing cravats; it is difficult to tell, as they
all have the same distinctive smell of turpentine and
lavender water.

The Queen endures this pantomime with remarkably
good grace. Although sometimes I notice her foot tapping
away beneath her robe (if the pose allows it).

Happily, it has been many years since there was any
suggestion that we should be subjected to a similar ordeal.

Back in 1986 old Geordie (Kelpie's great-great-uncle) had to perch on the Queen's knee for weeks on end while some grey-haired old man in a cravat struggled to capture his likeness.

The result was lamentable. He quite failed to convey the black smudge on Geordie's nose, and the ear tufts (which are such a distinctive feature of pedigree corgis) were sketched-in in the most perfunctory fashion.

When the idea for a corgi portrait was brought up again the other day (by the Queen Mother) it was dropped almost immediately, thank goodness. To have to sit still for any length of time, only to receive an unsatisfactory picture would have been too much of an imposition.

And yet HRH endures just that with horrible regularity. What an amazing woman she is.

⚜ Doctors ⚜

The Queen – and, indeed, the whole Royal Family – show a remarkable enthusiasm for unconventional or 'alternative' medicine. They never travel anywhere without a little black suitcase of homeopathic pills and potions.

The Queen Mother once fed us some of these little black pills inadvertently, mistaking them, I suppose, for chocolate drops. They tasted of seaweed and dried wood-bark: quite disgusting. Fib was violently sick after bolting down three of the things.

I remarked that a 'medicine' that made one ill was decidedly unsatisfactory. But Swift (who had overheard the Duke of Edinburgh expounding the subject to a party of East Anglian primary-school teachers) explained that that was, in fact, the whole idea behind homeopathic medicine.

I don't think anyone had taken the trouble to explain this

interesting fact to the under-footman who had to clean up
Fib's puddle of sick. He made several very ill-mannered and
ill-judged comments about corgis, carpets and alternative
medicine, which I shall not set down here.

The whole idea

PART SEVEN

State Visits

Scarcely hospitable

tate visits are always times of excitement at the Palace: the bunting is out and everyone is on their best behaviour. It is little wonder that visitors are often overawed by the splendour of the Royal Household.

❧   *The Reagans*   ❧

Ronald and Nancy Reagan were a dear old couple. They spent their visit wandering around the Palace wide-eyed with wonder, exclaiming 'My! How quaint!' almost continuously.

Mrs Reagan was most particularly wide-eyed. Indeed, she appeared to have undergone some ingenious operation to allow her eyes to stay stretched wide at all times.

The excitement of the visit had a pronounced effect upon Mr Reagan. He was frequently overcome by tiredness. Sometimes he even contrived to fall asleep while talking.

Mrs Reagan was alarmingly thin (and Fib, I am afraid to say, kept eyeing her bones greedily, which was scarcely hospitable). But she had considerably more energy than her husband. She entertained a constant stream of hairdressers, make-up artists, dress designers, clairvoyants and estate agents in her rooms.

I'm not sure, but it may have been Mrs Reagan who suggested to Fergie that she should move into a blue plastic pyramid.

❧ *President Mitterand* ❧

The French premier was a popular guest, certainly amongst the corgis. When it came to generosity with surreptitious morsels delivered discreetly to us under the table he was surpassed only by Princess Diana herself.

At one lunch a whole plateful of roast lamb (with mint sauce) was unobtrusively passed on to us with the well-known French exhortation to tuck in – '*Sacre Bleu! C'est immangeable.*' The operation was carried out with great deftness. It was a difficult blind manoeuvre as M. Mitterand did not want to draw attention to his generosity by leaning down to look under the table.

He managed the whole thing very well, although not without the occasional hiccup when his hand – reaching

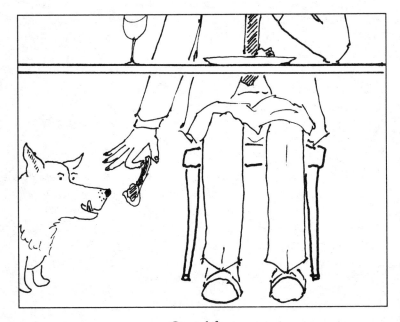

Great deftness

down to scratch our heads – would stray accidentally on to the knee of the lady on his right.

❧ *Mr Keating* ❧

With the Queen's great love of the Commonwealth we get many interesting visitors to the Palace from far distant countries. Recently we entertained the Australian Prime Minister, Mr Keating. The visit, however, despite the evident good will on both sides, was not an unqualified success.

Obviously a great lover of the monarchy, Mr Keating spent much of his time trying to put his arm around the Queen. This good-natured familiarity did not go down well with the Duke of Edinburgh. Ever the jealous male, he kept muttering darkly about 'the Lizard of Oz' and threatening to fetch his horsewhip.

Mr Keating became understandably nervous. He spent the rest of his visit eyeing the clock (a hideous piece of over-ornate ormulu work). No doubt he was trying to gauge the first moment that he could politely make his excuses and depart.

We haven't seen him again since that visit (and I'm not sure whether we've seen the antique ormulu carriage-clock either).

❧ *Euro-Royals* ❧

Occasionally we receive visits from the various slim-line, low-profile Royal Families of other European countries. These slim, trim, no-profile monarchs arrive on their bicycles from Belgium, Holland, Denmark, Norway, Spain or Hampstead

Garden Suburb for a kitchen-dinner and a chance to discuss such pressing topics as the role of the monarchy in the EC, where to get one's crown jewels reset, or the editorial policy of *Hello* – anything, indeed, except Gibraltar.

❧ *Sir Bob and Lady Geldof* ❧

I well remember the occasion of Sir Bob and Lady Geldof's visit to the Palace. Although it was, I have to confess, an evening tinged with disappointment.

In the run up to the party, the Duke of Edinburgh had constantly referred to the couple as 'that pair of dogs'. And, although the Duke is apt to employ jocular slang when talking about his guests, I really did suppose that we were in for some company.

After all, the name 'Sir Bob' sounded curiously familiar: I was sure that the winner of the All-England Sheep-Dog Trials in 1987 was called 'Sir Bob' – or something very like it.

As a result, the other corgis and I were looking forward to an evening of tail-wagging, bottom-sniffing and general carpet-capering; a chance to meet and mix with some 'ordinary' dogs.

Our hopes were raised another notch when, on the evening in question, we heard noises in the corridor outside the royal drawing-room. The sounds grew louder. 'Ah, that must be them now,' said the Duke, putting down his copy of *Polo Monthly.*

The noises were raucous and indistinct. There was a resonant growling bark, that went something like 'Fokking-fok-fok-fok', and was powerfully reminiscent of an Irish wolf-hound we had once met on the moors above Balmoral.

And then, cutting through this bass lilt, we heard the

piercing and incomprehensible 'Yip-yip-yip' which is the invariable signature tune of the miniature pekinese. 'That must be Lady G,' said Fib complacently. 'I didn't know she was a peke.'

What excitement: a wolf-hound and a pekinese. And coming specially to see us. What tales they might be able to tell of Irish bogs and Chelsea boudoirs. Or so we thought.

There was nothing to raise a doubt in our minds. For, by this stage, my quivering nose seemed to have confirmed the evidence of our ears. The deliciously fetid aroma of damp, matted hair, peat and whiskey, which one associates with the wolf-hound family was already overpowering the subtler scent of the Floris Special Reserve pot-pourri on the royal sideboard.

And behind the first pungent aroma there came a heady gust of cheap scent and raging pheromones. This was enough to set Fib off into a cacophony of over-excitement.

'Quiet,' said the Duke sternly. 'Here are our guests.' The door opened and the footman ushered in, not two fine pedigree dogs, but an ill-kempt shambling yob and a peroxide-headed trollop.

It took a moment for our eyes to register this disappointment. (The shambling yob did, after all, look very like a wolf-hound.) But we were soon obliged to admit our error: Sir Bob and Lady G were people. They had not been invited to meet us. They had come to see the Queen.

They all seemed to get on very well. The Duke kept recommending his barber to Sir Bob in a friendly (if rather insistent) fashion. And we had a happy enough time hoovering up the crumbs that Sir Bob thoughtfully spread over the carpet. Nevertheless, despite these consolations, the whole evening wore for me and the other corgis a definite air of anticlimax.

❧ *President Ceauşescu* ❧

Of all the state visits, however, the one I remember with the greatest fondness is that of President Ceauşescu and his dear wife. The Duke of Edinburgh, even now, goes red with pleasure when he recalls the happy event. And if he had a tail I'm sure he would wag it.

It was not that the visit was without its problems, but Mr Ceauşescu's unfailing courtesy and good humour surmounted every obstacle and made everyone grateful for his presence.

Almost as soon as he arrived and was shown into the Belgian Suite (which is always reserved for official visitors), the ever alert President thought that he had spotted a bug (probably brought in on the back of Princess Anne's mangy rottweiler during one of its happily rare visits).

It must have been a flea and it must have been hopping madly, because the President was soon springing about looking for it everywhere – in the light-fittings, the telephone mouthpiece, even the vase of flowers beside his bed.

Mr Ceauşescu was clearly placed in a difficult position: one does not expect to find fleas in a palace. But he was too much of a gentleman to mention the incident to his hosts. Instead he confided the facts (in diplomatically hushed tones) to one of his personal aides.

This gentleman then launched his own thorough search of the light-fittings, telephone mouthpiece and bedside flowers, but with the same lack of success. So Mr Ceauşescu and his aides all wore a wary expression for the rest of their stay, ever on the alert for the possible reappearance of the irritating bug.

The most considerate of guests, Ceauşescu would forbid his entourage to speak above a whisper inside the

Palace, even in their own suite, for fear of disturbing the Queen. Instead he would lead his fellow countrymen down to the bottom of the garden to discuss tedious affairs of state, where they wouldn't upset the Palace staff or the Royal Family.

Wanting to immerse himself in the British spirit, and to emulate the example of Princess Margaret, he took to drinking whisky at every meal – and, indeed, between every meal.

Mr Ceauşescu's enthusiasm for Scotch was immense. In an effort to raise awareness of the product back in Romania – and, no doubt, in the hope of promoting future trade in the stuff between Britain and his own country – he even removed several cases of ten-year-old single malt from the Palace cellars to take with him at the end of his stay.

The Queen, as a mark of her respect and admiration for this charming man, enrolled him in the Order of the Bath. She also, for a going-home present, gave him a beautiful hunting-rifle.

'I'd like to show him how it works,' said the Duke of Edinburgh with characteristic generosity and good humour.

It was obvious, however, that President Ceauşescu knew how it worked already. He seemed keen to try it out on several members of his own entourage. But his wife suggested that perhaps he had better wait until they all got home.

⚜ *Canine Visitors* ⚜

While the Queen receives regular visits from foreign Heads of State, it has to be said that we corgis are seldom graced with the same favour. If the Pope has a dog (and he certainly smelled as if he might), he did not think to bring it with him on his trip to England.

There are, however, exceptions. I remember well one thoughtful African president who arrived at the Palace with his two large hunting dogs.

I suppose he intended to introduce his beloved charges to us as a surprise, because he smuggled them first into the country (in a sort of 'diplomatic kennel'), and then into the Palace (in a large laundry basket). He had them closeted with him in the Belgian Suite and, in order to revive them after the rigours of the journey, he ordered several platefuls of raw steak from the Palace kitchens.

The ignorant kitchen staff (and I'm afraid to report that the level of ignorance amongst domestics is rising all the time) assumed that the raw steak was for the President's own breakfast. I, however, had my doubts from the first.

As soon as news leaked out that raw steak was being prepared below stairs, the other corgis and I were gathered by the green baize door awaiting its appearance. When the footman emerged bearing his precious cargo we followed him along the corridor, barking encouragement, until we arrived outside the Belgian Suite.

The noise was deafening: our own happy barks, the sound of the television blaring full volume, the strange wailing of some holy man (part of the President's entourage), the beat of drums. And yet through this din of distraction I could detect the unmistakable aroma of *dog*.

Well, of course, we redoubled our efforts at this discovery. Forgetting about the raw steak, we embarked (no pun intended) upon a vociferous hymn of welcome for our canine guests. And soon we could hear their responsive echo – deep and resonant, and strongly suggestive of the jungle.

At that moment, however, the footman, who was still preparing himself to knock on the door of the suite, let out some incoherent expletive, dropped the dish of steak, and dashed off down the corridor.

This was an unexpected bonus, but by the time we had polished off the raw meat the footman had returned with several guardsmen and a large net. They disappeared into the Belgian Suite, shouting a traditional African greeting which sounded rather like 'Rabiesalert!'

They emerged soon afterwards carrying a large laundry basket which they whisked off down the service stairs at such speed that we did not have time to inspect it. But I fear it must have contained our overseas visitors, for the powerful canine smell gradually faded from the corridor outside the Belgian Suite; the sonorous barks no longer answered our calls; and no more orders for raw steak were received in the kitchen.

Perhaps they had got bad news from home and had been obliged to leave hurriedly. Anyway it was a great shame that we never got to meet them.

I think HRH sensed our disappointment as, later that day, I heard her speaking quite crossly to the President about the whole debacle. 'Just think of the poor corgis,' she told him.

Another visiting dignitary who showed us a great deal of kindly attention was a small gentleman from – I believe – South Korea. He kept picking us up, patting our stomachs and pinching our flanks in a playful way, remarking, 'Good dog, nice dog.'

The Queen was delighted by this show of interest and remarked complacently, 'I see you are very fond of dogs.'

'Oh yes, your Majesty,' he replied, with that slightly shaky command of English which often enlivens state visits, 'I have one every day.'

The answer made no real sense, so the Queen merely smiled and poured more tea.

It was at that moment that some aftershave-scented courtier (seconded from the Foreign Office) leant over and whispered something in her ear. It was obviously grave news

– an international incident of some sort, involving South Korea, I can only suppose – because the Queen changed colour, sprang up, wrenched Swift from the Oriental dignitary's grasp and quickly ushered all of us corgis out of the room. Clearly there was serious and disturbing business to be discussed.

Such rude interruptions of diplomatic necessity into the gracious flow of domestic pleasure are amongst the drawbacks of life in the Royal Household. It was a shame that we didn't get a chance to get to know our Korean friend better, or to wish him goodbye more formally. We never saw him again.

PART EIGHT

The Corgi's Year

Celebration, pageantry and pomp

❦ *The Trooping of The Colour* ❦

The second Saturday in June is always a very special occasion: the Queen's Official Birthday, a time of celebration, pageantry and pomp. The main focus of the great day is, of course, the so-called Trooping of the Colour. It is not commonly realised, however, that this event is divided into two parts.

There is the great public jamboree on the Horseguards Parade and, until very recently, the Queen would ride around on her horse in her full regimental rig, while the crowds waved tiny plastic Union Jacks – and sad attention-seeking republicans fired blank cartridges at her.

Less well-known, however, was the small private ceremony that used to precede it. This event, which was laid on for the benefit of the corgis (and the kitchen staff), is considered by all who have witnessed it to be the real core of the Birthday celebrations. It is sad to find it discontinued.

The ritual was simple yet dramatic. The Queen, mounted side-saddle on her faithful horse, Burmese, and dressed in the scarlet uniform of one of her many regiments, would ride around the Palace gardens, while the corgis pursued her barking furiously, and the kitchen servants lined the pathways beating pots and pans and cheering wildly. It was a splendid scene, full of a vitality and joy that the public spectacle rarely matched.

I have heard some of the stuffier courtiers suggesting that this ceremony was merely laid on to accustom Burmese to the noise she would face once she left the Palace precincts. But this is nonsense. It was a celebration of the corgi's place at the heart of the Royal Household, a chance for us to sport with our monarch on the greatest day in her calendar.

It used to be a very wonderful sight (and sound) and it is only a pity that more people have not been privileged to witness it. Instead the general public still has to make do with over two hours of intricate formation marching.

⚜ Garden Parties ⚜

July is the month of Royal Garden Parties. These annual bun-fights, at Buckingham Palace or Holyrood House, are a great opportunity for us to practise our herding techniques.

We operate on a simple colour-coding system. First we

An opportunity for practice

round up all the bishops and antipodean musical artistes (all recognisable by their bright purple vestments) into one group. Then we gather in all the full-blown county matrons (in blue). And finally we tackle the vast herd of people in special ill-fitting morning coats with overtight shirt-collars.

It is a difficult business, as half the throng cluster excitedly about Princess Diana as soon as she makes an appearance, while the rest wander off in every direction to steal plants from the more distant corners of the garden.

Plant-stealing is quite a recent phenomenon. In the old days people merely stole the tea spoons.

❧ *Charles's Fortieth Birthday Bash* ❧

I always enjoy a do. Every corgi does. The Garden Parties are wonderful events in their way, but rather too diffuse. More agreeable to my way of thinking are the splendid extravaganzas sometimes held inside the Palace.

One of the finest of these was the bash organised by Prince Edward for Prince Charles's fortieth birthday. Preparations were in train for weeks. Corgis are very swift to detect plans for change: favourite chairs are moved, favourite carpets are rolled up and put away.

An air of pre-occupation and bustle seems to envelop all the human inhabitants of the Palace. This has its virtues as well as its inconveniences. Doors get left open, lunch trolleys stand unattended. In the week running up to a big party it is quite possible to treble one's daily food intake. And on the party night itself everyone is far too busy to notice what one is up to.

For Charles's fortieth the Picture Gallery was hung with a vast tent brought over from Saudi Arabia by some rather unfriendly gentlemen dressed in their own personal tents.

We kept trying to introduce ourselves to these exotic-looking persons (close friends of Prince Charles's) but they would shy away in alarm, shouting 'Unclean, unclean.' And this when we had been bathed within the week.

The guest list included many old friends, so we were much feted and treated to numerous little snacks. One of the great virtues of buffet dining is that people seem to find it almost impossible to hold on to a glass and serve themselves even the simplest of foods without spillages.

I stationed myself under the breakfast buffet and was able to feast throughout the small hours on the scatter of kidneys, scrambled egg, bacon rashers and croissant crumbs.

Fib was brought close to feeding-frenzy by the opportunities on offer. In his excitement he started devouring discarded napkins, valuable rugs, the hem of the tent, the train of Princess Margaret's dress, and some of the thick black cables that snaked across the floor behind the makeshift stage.

At midnight a bald, diminutive Cockney, who Prince Charles referred to graciously as, 'That nice man, Philip Collins', appeared on stage to begin his celebrated mime show.

These sort of things are not my particular interest, but it was obviously a great success. As Mr Collins stood there silently gesticulating under the arc lights everyone laughed uproariously. Everyone, that is, except Prince Edward.

Indeed the young Prince – although he was standing in the audience – appeared to be part of the act. First of all he went very red and then he started waving his arms about. It was an energetic display, marred only by the fact that he broke the sacred tenet of mime by speaking, or rather shouting.

'Crikey,' he yelped, 'the sound system's gone down.'

This sally was greeted with cheers in some quarters.

'Hooray,' shouted the Duke of Edinburgh.

'What a relief,' beamed HRH.

Others, however, are less easily amused. Princess Diana, obviously a stern critic of this sort of alternative cabaret, actually stamped her foot and hissed to the amiable cavalry officer at her side, 'It's pathetic, they couldn't organise a piss-up in a brewery.'

Her dashing friend very properly reprimanded her for this uncharitable – and unfestive – remark by pinching her bottom. She wriggled uncomfortably and whispered something to him that I didn't catch. She was obviously still complaining, however, because her escort felt obliged to administer a second deft pinch as a follow-up to the initial punishment. Thank heavens for military discipline.

After that the dumb-show ended and the music started up. This is always the signal for the corgis to leave the room. Music affects people very strangely. They lose all sense of balance and co-ordination; they set off across the floor, determined to trample on anything and everything in their path.

For the most part they concentrate their energies on stepping upon each others' feet, but they will happily clump on a sequined dress-train, a discarded croissant or, unfortunately, a corgi.

We made our escape in a phalanx and sought sanctuary in a distant drawing-room where the Queen Mother was reclining on a sofa eating liqueur chocolates.

'Ah,' she said, welcoming us with her usual expansive warmth. 'At last, someone to talk to.'

Royal Ascot

A day at the races is an exciting diversion. The colour, the crowd, the discarded half-eaten hamburgers, the sweet smell of the horse manure: everything is fun.

Nevertheless, an outing to Ascot, although enjoyable in itself, always leaves me with the uncomfortable sensation that the corgi may not – after all – be the Queen's favourite animal. We have a rival: the horse.

The Queen gets very excited by horses. She talks about them intently to her racing manager (at least that's what I suppose they are talking about), she pores over their finer points, she analyses their form, all with a diligence and application which she only rarely lavishes on us, her faithful dogs.

Of course she doesn't pet her horses (so much), nor does she allow them to sit under the table at lunch. But when they are racing she follows their progress with an enthusiasm and intensity which contrasts rather sharply with her much more relaxed interest in our own fiercely competitive canine races and games on the lawns at Balmoral.

Nevertheless, by the end of the day, when we are safely back at Windsor or the Palace, and we have relived for the last time the closing stages of some race, we know that it will be with us that HRH settles down for the evening.

It will be we who receive the indulgent scratch under the chin, the piece of breadstick under the table, while the horses are led away in draughty and uncomfortable-looking boxes. It is a consoling vision.

❧ *Polo* ❧

One of the diversions of weekend life at Windsor is the Polo on Smith's Lawn. Polo is a good spectator sport for corgis with numerous over-dressed spectators in high-heeled shoes to be nipped at and herded about.

The annual International Day in August has become the key event in the social calendar. It is a jolly occasion. There is usually plenty of good food littering the grass around the aptly named hospitality tents. Kind-hearted businessmen with red-faces and bulging waistlines thoughtfully scatter chicken drumsticks and sausage rolls from their paper plates.

The game itself, however, remains a complete mystery. It involves, as far as I can tell, three distinct groups: pink-faced British military types smelling of sweat, small swarthy Argentines smelling of expensive cologne, and small swarthy ponies smelling of warm hay.

One of the arcane pre-match rituals seems to involve players putting a hand down their jodhpurs and 'rearranging' themselves. Prince Charles is obviously very good at this particular manoeuvre. Indeed, there are post-cards of him executing it in almost every newsagent in Windsor.

Princess Di has, I think, been watching him closely, and – having mastered the knack herself – is now keen to pass it on to others. Fib told me that he came across the Princess in an empty horsebox instructing one of her young cavalry officer friends in the delicate operation.

State Opening of Parliament

November always sees the State Opening of Parliament. It is not an event I have ever attended. Nor have I any desire to. Its manifestations within the Palace are quite enough to be gong on with.

At the beginning of the month a whole suite of ceremonial robes is dragged from some long-locked wardrobe. The Queen's chambers reek of mothballs for days.

As the Royal dressers busy themselves with stitching on gold braid and ermine trim, the floor soon becomes littered with dangerous pins. It is not safe to lie anywhere.

The whole operation, moreover, is not helped by Fib who – ever on the alert for interloping mice – is always seizing hold of fur scraps and worrying them vigorously. And no sooner does he begin this ermine-worrying act than all the dressers, as one, leap on to their chairs and start shrieking.

The calm of Palace existence is quite destroyed for well over a week. And all for what?

Christmas

Christmas means Sandringham: cold floors, bad draughts and family squabbles. (Although it can mean Balmoral: family squabbles, bad draughts and cold floors.)

Christmas, as everyone remarks, gets earlier each year. Indeed I have even noticed that people have started making this observation earlier each year.

The Queen starts writing out her Xmas cards towards the end of July so that they will reach the far-flung corners of the Commonwealth in time for the great day. The last posting date for Christmas mail to the August Bank Holiday Islands is the August bank holiday.

But the first really palpable sign of the approaching festivities is the arrival of a group of men in sleeveless Puffa-jackets bearing arc-lights and yards of electric flex.

According to the Duke of Edinburgh they come to perform 'that ridiculous charade we have to go through each year'. Certainly the charade does seem rather ridiculous (and not up to the usual standard of Royal theatricals). For a start it is always the same. The Queen sits behind her desk with her spectacles on, while the men in Puffa-jackets shine their lights in her face.

Moreover, although HRH has been doing the same charade for years, no one has ever been able to guess what the hidden word might be. As far as I can make out it must be 'Commonwealth', but no one seems to have suggested this.

After the annual ritual has been completed preparations are then made for our departure to the country. The staff at Buckingham Palace are always very sad to see us go. And there is usually a big send-off party for us.

The Servants' Hall is awash with drink and festooned with paper-chains. The servants themselves, in a touching show of loyal emotion, often burst into tears at this event. Some are so overcome with feeling that they fall over. A few, brought to heart-rending extremes of misery, are actually sick. And all this even though we are only going away for a few weeks.

The Queen is understandably moved by such displays. Until quite recently she used to dance with one or two of the servants as a mark of her affection or regard. But this often proved too much for them. They would stagger under the burden of pleasure and excitement. HRH, not infrequently, was in danger of having her toes crushed or her dress torn.

In recent years it has been considered wiser to dispense

The real joy of Christmas

with the dancing. Now the Queen merely passes amongst her loyal staff, waving and offering words of Xmas cheer.

After this touching scene we all head off to Sandringham (if not Balmoral) for Christmas proper.

The Queen's Christmas regime has become well-established over the years: church in the morning, lunch and then charades and present-giving.

We don't attend church (the flagstone floor is far too cold) and lunch is a disappointment; Christmas scraps are largely made up of Brussels sprouts – not a favourite of mine or, it seems, anyone else. The charades, however, are fun.

As a warm-up the Queen always insists that everyone tries one more time to guess the 'ridiculous charade' that she performed at the palace in the weeks before Christmas. She has it specially broadcast on the television. We all have to traipse through to the red drawing-room and gather round the large Korean teak television cabinet, while the Duke of Edinburgh fiddles with the aerial. Even though we have all had weeks to think about it, no one is ever able to come up with a convincing explanation as to what it is all about. The Queen, however, never seems to mind.

Afterwards there are further charades and theatricals, usually involving rather more interaction and dressing-up, with Prince Edward always in the vanguard, putting on powdered wigs, silk crinolines, silly voices and electric kettles, and urging his siblings to do likewise.

But, of course, the real joy of Christmas is the presents. All corgis love discarded wrapping paper. It is perfect for frolicking about in – almost as good as autumn leaves (although, alas, without the possibility of coming across any concealed dog-mess).

By the end of the day we – along with the rest of the family – are in that state of exhausted over-excitement mingled with mild nausea which is the essential flavour of a Happy Christmas.

Epilogue

As I look back over the long cold summer during which I have been composing these memoirs it seems to me that the Royal Family may be entering upon a new and happier phase of existence.

There is an unaccustomed serenity about the Palace: no Fergie crashing about to her early morning work-out video; no Princess Diana precipitating herself into the glass-fronted display cases; no Major Ron playing carpet polo with the fire irons. Things may be duller but they are certainly calmer.

The Royal Corgis have been touched by this general mood of tranquillity. We, too, are entering upon a new and happier phase of existence. The recent arrival of some bespoke hand-crafted dog-baskets has greatly increased the comforts of home life.

The baskets, raised off the ground on short legs, keep one nicely out of the draught. And they provide too an excellent vantage point from which to view the unfolding royal pageant of the coming years. Long may it continue.

GOD SAVE THE QUEEN

Index